The Field Guide *to* Dumb Birds
of North America

The Field Guide *to* Dumb Birds *of* North America

Matt Kracht

CHRONICLE BOOKS
SAN FRANCISCO

Library of Congress Cataloging-in-Publication Data available.
ISBN 978-1-4521-7403-7

Manufactured in China.

Design by Jenna Huerta

Chronicle Books LLC
680 Second Street
San Francisco, CA 94107

www.chroniclebooks.com

20 19 18 17 16 15

Contents

Introduction

Quite a few people have asked me how I came to write about birds, and this is the story I tell them:

I was first introduced to bird watching when I was in the fourth grade. My teacher was an amateur ornithologist and a total nut for birds. Our class went on bird watching field trips. We read about birds. We watched nature documentaries about birds. And we each had to write a *Bird Report* about a specific bird over Christmas break.

I argued for the black-capped chickadee (I liked them, and they're everywhere in the Pacific Northwest where I live) but was ultimately assigned the golden-crowned kinglet. These things are nearly impossible to spot: they're tiny, they hang out in the deep woods, and they don't want to be anywhere near a fourth grader.

I spent countless hours in the cold, dripping November woods and the knee-high grass of marshy fields with the dew soaking through my shoes trying to spot a golden-crowned kinglet so I could write my observations for the report. I never saw one. Maybe I saw one once in a tree. But it might have been a pinecone. Impossible to tell at that distance.

The *Bird Report* was the first real report I ever had to write. It was also my first experience with crushing academic anxiety. On the last day of Christmas vacation, I cried because I didn't know how to begin writing about a bird I had never seen in reality. Vacation was over, there was no time left, and I was paralyzed by impending failure. In the end, my mom made me hunker down and do it anyway.

When I was finished, I had a blue cardboard report binder titled, *Bird Report*, which held the meager collection of handwritten pages and drawings that I was able to eke out in one long evening of despair spent with an encyclopedia and a field guide borrowed from the library. It was C- material at best.

Fast-forward three and a half decades. Life is great and I'm taking a nice New Year's Day walk with my wife along the shore of the Puget Sound near our home. The air is crisp, the water is lapping at the shore, the wind is rustling in the trees, and the sun is shining. Then I see it—not three feet away in the bushes at the edge of the woods—unmistakable: *The Golden Crowned Kinglet!* I couldn't believe it. It was literally within arm's reach.

I froze and pointed it out to my wife. "*Look*," I whispered loudly, "*a golden-crowned kinglet!*"

I carefully pulled my phone from my pocket to snap a picture of it—proof of achievement for an assignment I suddenly realized had felt incomplete for nearly forty years. But that tiny little fucker would not stop jumping from spot to spot, barely landing in the branches of a bush for a split second before it flitted away behind a leaf or into some tall grass, each time before I could find it and my camera could focus on it. It was like trying to capture photographic evidence of Bigfoot.

"Pretty," my wife said when it finally flew away into the trees, and we walked on.

"*You little son of a bitch*," I thought. The rest is history.

Golden Crowned Kinglet
Seattle, Jan 1st 2017

Section I:

How to use this book

If you are new to bird watching, you may benefit from familiarizing yourself with this guide and its different parts, especially the part with the birds in it. In addition to a drawing of the bird, each entry includes a description of physical appearance and notes on its behavior, calls, and general disposition. These are intended to aid not only with proper identification, but to help you on your way to a deeper understanding and appreciation of how truly horrible these tiresome little creatures are.

Beyond the descriptions of birds, you will find information in this book covering many topics of interest to the bird watcher, including the history of bird watching, methods of identification, where to look for birds, tips for bird watching, seasonal bird watching and, if you are inclined to follow your new obsession to an even deeper place, how to observe and record birds in your own journal.

Additionally, in the back you will find maps pertaining to bird regions of North America and seasonal migratory patterns across the continent, as well as illustrations and descriptions of the different kinds of bird feeders that attract birds to yards.

If you are like me, the observation of birds may well become a lifetime distraction and ultimately provide you with countless hours of profound irritation.

If, on the other hand, you are already an experienced bird watcher, I'm sorry.

The Difference Between Birding and Bird Watching

Until recently there was no debate over the difference between the terms, because rational people generally agreed that you can't just turn a noun into a verb just because you feel like it, and thus the terms "birding" and "birder" did not exist. Sadly, those days are over.

Exactly how and when the chain of events leading to the present debate was set in motion is impossible to say, but it almost certainly started with some early 19th century drip staring at a tree for hours with his mouth agape. When a passing acquaintance asked him what he was up to, he probably said, "What? Oh, I was watching a bird," and was subsequently ridiculed for wasting time watching a common bird doing bird things. This no doubt led him to decide, "I had better say *'I am bird watching'* the next time, because that sounds like I'm doing something serious."

Fast-forward a hundred years or so to a drawing room after a dinner party, and we can only assume that essentially the same language evolution happened again. Someone said approvingly to the host, "Those are some splendid binoculars! Perfect for safari, I'd say. I didn't know you hunted, old boy!" To which this host surely must have stammered out, "I . . . they're for, um, bird watching," and then, to make it sound a bit more dangerous, and to hopefully dodge the loss of his big-game-hunting peer's newfound admiration, he quickly added, "that is to say, *birding*. Yes, ha ha, I'm a big *birder*." This was no doubt followed by an awkward silence and the subject was quickly changed to who would care for a brandy.

During the 20th century the observation of birds as a pastime grew rapidly in popularity and became a hobby enjoyed casually even by common people.

At some point a bunch of Type As decided to make the watching of birds even more unenjoyable by declaring that the whole point of it was going to be who can see the most birds in the course of their overcompetitive lifetime.

Many birders feel that "bird watching" is a passive activity, whereas what they do (rushing around trying to see every single bird and write it down) is an active activity, which is why it needs its own more active verb-noun to describe it. Because they're not passively *watching* birds, they're actively *birding* birds.

It makes sense to them, I guess. Regardless, while these obsessive bird-listers weren't the first to call themselves "birders," they've certainly owned the term in recent years, at least in their minds.

Today, in reality, the two terms are for the most part used interchangeably by laypeople, and the only substantive difference between a "birder" and a "bird watcher" is the degree of pretentious erudition versus competitive prick-ness.

If you're wondering which camp I fall in, it's neither—people watch birds for many reasons; it may be for the bragging rights, the love of nature, or just to feel less boring, but that's not why I do it. I am a professional bird critic.

Where to Look for Birds

Birds are more or less every-goddamned-where you look. Whether you want them to be or not, once you start looking, they're all over the place. But if you still need some help, here are a few suggestions on where to find them:

1. Obviously, out in nature. If you don't immediately spot one in the air, you can find them in trees, in bushes, on the ground, floating in water, etc. If you don't see them, try listening, because they're frequently making a bunch of noise and ruining the peaceful quietness of nature. Nature is basically infested with birds.

2. Your backyard. Because birds are too dumb to know the difference between your backyard and nature.

3. The city. People often think of birds living in the woods, or frolicking in suburban birdbaths, but one look at the mess on any bus stop bench will prove otherwise. Watch where you sit.

4. Virtually the whole world. From one pole to the other—in climates hot and cold, the desert, by the sea, a tropical landscape, you name it—in nearly every environment on this planet: *birds*. I'm telling you, there's no getting away from them.

How to Identify Birds

The first step in correctly identifying which dumb bird you are looking at is knowing the basic bird parts. The sparrow is a good example; it's very boring, but it has the basic "bird" shape, and trust me, they all have pretty much the same parts.

Head: You can probably figure this one out on your own, but it's generally the thing on top of the bird. It's one of the best places to look for the eyes and the beak, which can also help you with identification.

Field markings may include the crown (top of the head), the nape (back of the head), eye-rings, eye-lines, and supposedly, eyebrows.

Bill or Beak: No one knows what the difference between a bill and a beak is, but the shape and size is pretty important if you're trying to identify a bird. Always pay close attention to this part, because this is what they will peck you blind with, if you give them half a chance.

Chin: This may often be hard to see on a bird, as most birds are weak-chinned. This suggests they have a weak personality and may lack the willpower to follow projects through to completion.

Throat: Between the chin and the chest. This is where all that goddamn noise comes from.

Neck: Most birds don't have a neck, or at least not one you can see, because it's typically very short. On the other hand, many wading birds have extremely long necks, which may be a good place to look for identifying markings on these gangly looking sons of bitches. Short or long, one thing you are never going to see is a bird with a normal-length neck.

Back: This is the back of the bird. Try to familiarize yourself with the back markings of as many species as possible, because most birds are assholes and have no problem sitting with their backs to you and ignoring you like you don't even matter.

Chest: Also referred to as the breast. Can be difficult to cook without drying it out.

Abdomen: Goes from the breast down to the undertail. Also called the belly, but not by anyone who's worth taking seriously.

Flanks: This is ornithologist-speak for the sides of a bird. What a bunch of a-holes. Just call it the sides.

Wings: Seriously, I'm not even going to explain this one. This is the part that makes it a bird.

Rump: The rump is the patch between the back and the tail. Basically, it's the lower back. For most birds, the rump doesn't really stand out. But a few species do have unique rump colorations that could be helpful, if you somehow managed to not be able to make an identification based on the clues from the entire rest of the bird.

Tail: This is the part that sticks off the back of the bird. A multitude of shapes, lengths, and colors make the tail invaluable in identification. Even how the tail is held can tell an observant watcher a lot about a bird. *"Tail up, stuck up,"* is what I always say.

Vent: It's also called the cloaca, but don't let the fancy anatomical terminology fool you; this is the butthole. Birds shit whenever they feel like it, and also whenever they are above your vehicle.

· Just venting: Did you know that in addition to excretion, the cloaca is also used for laying eggs? Gross.

Undertail Coverts: This is getting boring. These are the short feathers under the tail; they may have colors or markings that could distinguish between some species, but honestly, who's even looking?

Legs: Length, color, and even thickness can be useful for identification. If you want a good laugh some time, try imagining a bird with fat legs.

Feet: This is what they walk on when they're too lazy to fly.

· Foot Fact: Most birds' feet are the same color as their legs, but not all of them! So, if you see a bird from a distance and you think it might be wearing shoes, don't say anything, because a lot of ornithologists will never let you live this down.

Bird Size

Another attribute that may help you identify a bird is the size. This can be especially handy when you can't get a clear look at the field markings. When judging a bird's size, you may find it useful to practice comparing them to something familiar that is similar in size. For example, is this bird the size of your thumb, or more like your whole fist clutching a thumb-sized bird?

Bird Shape

Does it have a small body with long stupid legs, or is it dumpy with a fat head? While no two birds are the same, they come in six main bird shapes.

THE SIX MAIN
BIRD SHAPES

BASIC

LUMP

Shitsack

FLOATERS

WEIRD Legs

Murder

Bird Behaviors

Careful observation of behavior may provide additional clues when identifying birds. Does it sit erect with its tail straight down like a prim little prig, or does it hold its tail up, like it thinks it is better than everybody? Does it dart around on the ground endlessly like an excitable idiot, or does it waste everyone's time perching and singing all day? The behavior of a bird can tell you a lot about what kind of asshole you're dealing with.

Bird Songs and Calls

Bird *songs* are typically sung by the male. It's basically intended to warn other males away from its breeding territory, impress the females, and announce its availability for romance. In most species, the song is limited to the breeding season, because let's face it, if you know you're not going to get lucky all winter long, why waste your breath singing about it.

Bird *calls*, on the other hand are produced by both genders and tend to be unmusical, less complex, and serve more practical, non-sexy purposes such as location calls, warning sounds, and intimidation of others.

There is seemingly endless variety in the songs, calls, and noises in the world of birds, certainly more that we can cover here. Suffice to say, birds are noisy fuckers who just will not shut up.

Ethics

The first bird watchers may or may not have known that, fundamentally, the act of watching birds disturbs birds. If they did understand this, I'm pretty sure they didn't give two shits because if you're a 19th century naturalist, being sensitive to a bird's feelings is not your primary concern.

These days, however, many modern bird guides touch on the ethical observation of birds in the wild, which mainly consists of how to have as little impact on the birds as possible. Of course, no one ever mentions the fact that birds give no thought whatsoever to disturbing you at all hours of the day with their incessant flitting and chattering.

Really, the best way to avoid disturbing birds is to avoid birds all together. But if that is not possible, don't worry because here comes the American Birding Association. The ABA is widely accepted as the standard-bearer of birding for serious birders in the U.S. and Canada, and has put together their Code of Birding Ethics for you to follow. You can read the code in its entirety on the ABA website, but it is long and bossy, so I have summarized it below to save you the headache:

Section 1 is about the welfare of birds and their environment.

It's a lot of junk regarding the protection of bird habitats, and not stressing out the birds when you're busy watching, photographing, filming, and audio-recording them. Also, trying to be sensitive about terrorizing them as little as possible with the use of flashes and artificial lighting when you're shooting your close-ups. There's a bunch of other stuff, too, but TL;DR.

Section 2 is about not breaking the law.

Most people understand that you are not supposed to break the law, because this is one of the core tenets behind having laws in the first place. But the ABA felt that birders could use some extra lecturing about this, so they've laid out some helpful hints for anyone who needs a refresher in the basic rules of civilization. They cover all the classics like "do not enter private property without permission" and "follow all the rules and regulations governing the place where you are birding," and "have some courtesy for others while you're at it." The list goes on, but essentially, "don't be a trespasser or a dick."

Note: This is actually all pretty good advice, because it will generally keep you out of trouble with the police. However, don't expect birds to return the favor, as they lack civility and have no regard for the law.

Section 3 is about keeping it safe and clean.

This one is mostly about birdhouse upkeep, keeping food and water dispensers clean, and that sort of thing. Boring. Oh, there is also a point about how, if you're attracting birds to an area, you should make sure they're not exposed to predation by domestic animals. But come on—if you're putting a bird feeder in your yard in the first place, we all know it's going to get the neighborhood cats sharpening their claws.

Section 4 is about group birding and telling on other birders.

The first couple of items in this section stipulate that if you witness another birder engaged in any sort of unethical birding behavior, then you are supposed to document it and notify all of the appropriate individuals and organizations. Essentially, dime out anyone who breaks the rules of the code, like you are some sort of junior G-man on the case.

Then there are about five more points all detailing your sacred responsibilities if you are leading a group of bird watchers. Honestly, I would suggest bird watching alone if at all possible; birders are a weird bunch, and one of them (see above) is just waiting for you to make a mistake so they can report you and take over.

Author's Note:

The ABA asks that you please follow their code and distribute and teach it to others. If you can't be dissuaded from birding, or if you enjoy reading rules, I recommend that you visit the ABA website (aba.org) and read the official version in its entirety. As far as codes of birding ethics go, it is the gold standard.

All that said, for what it's worth, birds themselves are unethical little creeps. Take a look at their mating and child-rearing habits if you don't believe me. Plus, they don't even think twice before just plain shitting all over your Adirondack chairs.

Section 2:
The Birds

This is the part of the book with all the birds in it. If you're familiar with the major field guides, you know that there are a number of ways to categorize birds.

The most traditional guides follow taxonomic order, which is great if you're particularly stuffy, or an ornithologist. Other guides organize the birds in a more relaxed manner, like by family and species similarity. If you want to get really sloppy, there are even guides with birds arranged by physical characteristics like what shape they are or the size of their bill. This last approach may be incredibly useful when making a quick identification in the field, but believe me, there are some academics who are pursing their lips indignantly right now just thinking about it.

The birds in this guide are organized according to the type of bird they are deep down inside.

Typical Birds

American Goldfink

Common Name: American Goldfinch

Look at this handsome little fuck. His dazzling yellow plumage and glossy black markings really make him stand out at the backyard bird feeder, don't they? But then again, it's not that difficult to look good when your competition is a bunch of painfully drab siskins and dingy redpolls, is it, you conceited little dicks?

Colors: *Intense yellow and hey, everybody, look at me, look at me! I'm so striking.*

American
GoldFINK

Black-capped Prickadee

Common Name: Black-capped Chickadee

A lot of people consider this bird cute. Whatever. They are curious and have a habit of energetically investigating everything and everyone that might possibly be a bird feeder. Their black cap and white cheeks are almost as distinctive as their bright, "chickadee-dee-dee" call. And "Dee Dee Dee Dee!" And also, "DEE DEE DEE DEE DEE DEE DEEEEE!" And I mean nonstop. If you have these little pricks in your yard, you're getting no peace all summer.

Dee Facts: *The black-capped chickadee is a non-migratory bird, so you can forget about enjoying fall, winter, and spring, too.*

black-capped
prickadee

Bushtit

Common Name: Bushtit

Seriously, that's its actual name. There is nothing interesting about this drab tit.

Color: *Drab*

Bushtit

Dork-eye Junco

Common Name: Dark-eyed Junco

Sometimes described as attractive, or even "flashy," this twerp is actually just another gray American sparrow. But this doesn't stop it from flitting to and fro all over the forest floors, making its loud, painfully high-pitched trill, and scratching around for food with its feet.

The male's song is a loud trill of the same note, repeated up to 23 times. It can last for several seconds and is irritating enough to be heard from hundreds of feet away.

Color: *Boring. It's got a white under-belly, as if anyone cares.*

dork-eye
junco

Dumb Western Bluebird

Common Name: Western Bluebird

Guess what color this dumb bluebird bird is! Now that we've covered identification, let's talk about the real story here, which is that this bird is a loser. They are what's called a "cavity nester," which means they live in holes, but these schmucks can't even dig out their own holes because their beaks are too weak. They have to squat in abandoned woodpecker nests or whatever other hole they can find. Failing that, they move into man-made nest boxes, which are basically bird slums, where they're attacked by competing freeloaders like starlings and house sparrows. Then there are the raccoons, cats, possums, and various hawks who can't wait to fuck up a bluebird, or make off with an egg. Oh, and ants, bees, wasps, and earwigs all love to get into a bluebird-hole and cause problems for the young. Born. Loser.

Father Figures: *Western bluebirds appear to form monogamous pairs each year, but in genetic studies, 45% of nests had young that were not fathered by the male partner. Son of a bitch can't catch a break.*

dumb western
bluebird

Evening Grossbutt

Common Name: Evening Grosbeak

This fat-billed little chunk-of-finch is usually found in the northern coniferous forest, but during the winter you basically can't hide from it. They appear erratically all over North America and are well-known for descending on bird feeders in noisy flocks to demolish your supply of sunflower seeds without so much as a "thank you."

Genus loves company! *Did you know that the International Ornithologists' Union has this dumb grosbeak in the genus* Hesperiphona, *while the American Ornithological Society places it under the genus* Coccothraustes *(the same genus as the hawfinch)?!? Naturally, this raises the question, "Oh my god, how am I even still awake?"*

Evening Grossbutt

Golden Crowned Dumb-Shit

Common Name: Golden-crowned Kinglet

This dumb little shit just hops all over the place. In the trees. In the grass. In the bushes. Everywhere. Nonstop. It can't sit still for even one goddamned second so you could maybe take a picture of it that's not blurry or obscured by twigs. That's why I had to draw the little fuck instead. He has a stupid yellow stripe on his head.

golden crowned
dumb-shit

Goddamn Song Sparrow

Common Name: Song Sparrow

This sparrow gets its name from its repertoire of colorful songs—so colorful, some sparrow enthusiasts even say that one frequently heard song resembles the first three notes of *Ludwig van Beethoven's Symphony No. 5 . . .* Just think about that for a moment, because what the hell are you talking about? Beethoven's 5th opens with maybe the most recognizable four-note motif in orchestra music. Everybody knows it: "Duh-duh-duh DAHHHHHH!" The first three notes, however, are just "duh-duh-duh." That's also the opening motif of "Ice Ice Baby," so maybe you sparrow enthusiasts can put away your top hats and opera glasses and take it down a notch, okay?

In actual fact, these sparrows' songs vary greatly with region, and many can be quite complex, with multiple phrases and different trills added by the individual singer. This is probably an attempt to compensate for their looks

Identification: *Small, light brown with darker brown streaks. Looks like a beige ankle sock, if someone ran through the woods wearing it and slipped in mud.*

goddamn
Song
Sparrow

Gray Cat Turd

Common Name: Gray Catbird

This perching gray turd of the mimid family is a relative of mockingbirds and thrashers, but its scientific name, *dumetella carolinensis*, is based upon the Latin term *dumus*. Which, if you think about it, sounds a lot like *dumbass*.

Ornithologists invariably insist on mentioning the gray catbird's "catlike mew" call, but it makes you wonder how familiar they are with cats, because in reality it sounds a lot like a shrill bird. I guess maybe you *could* imagine the call was catlike, if that cat was very hoarse, and you surprised it by stepping on its tail.

Appearance: *Grayish-gray, with a reddish-brown butt. Bird-like.*

Did you know? *While the gray catbird eats a variety of worms and bugs, a full half of its diet is fruits and berries, so I'm thinking probably don't stand under one if you can avoid it.*

gray
cat turd

House Binch

Common Name: House Finch

These cheerful sons-of-finches were originally native to Mexico and the Southwestern United States, but they moved their way up the West Coast in the '50s and '60s. Since then they have spread to the East Coast. In fact, now they pretty much cover the entire continent. Oh, and Hawaii. They appear in noisy groups in city parks and suburban backyards nearly everywhere these days. Males sing a jumbled, rambling string of short warbled notes. No one can make any sense of it.

Identification: *Streaky gray and brown tail and abdomen. Males have rosy red smudges around the face and upper chest. Pretty fat beaks for such chubby little bodies.*

House
Binch

Kentucky Gargler

Common Name: Kentucky Warbler

This fuck lives in the deciduous forests of the southeastern United States. It is heavy and sluggish for a warbler, so it spends most of its time on the ground. It can fly when it wants to, but you're more likely to accidentally step on one than see it in the trees. The males consider themselves real singers and won't shut up.

Kentucky
~~Kentucky~~
Gargler

Lameland Longspur

Common Name: Lapland Longspur

Also called a "Lapland Bunting," this streaked brown sparrow is common in the Arctic tundra during the summer months when it is breeding and enjoying continual daylight and a rich diet of insects. Must be nice. Most of us are more likely to have seen it during the winter months, when they descend in huge flocks on the frozen farmlands of Canada and the northern United States, consuming vast quantities of whatever seeds and waste grain they can take from the already bleak fields. What did the Midwest ever do to them?

Flock Facts: *Winter flocks of these birds may be as large as four million, and they have been known to kill themselves by the thousands by flying into lighted structures like radio towers during winter storms. In 1904, during in a snowstorm in western Minnesota and Iowa, an estimated 1,500,000 of these dumbasses bought the farm this way. As if winter in the Midwest isn't horrible enough without millions of frozen bird carcasses littering the ground wherever tall structures are.*

L̶a̶m̶e̶ Land
Long Spur

Palm Burglar

Common Name: Palm Warbler

This rusty-capped member of the warbler family is easily
recognized by its tail-wagging habit, which shows off its yellow
undertail, or "ass," in an embarrassingly clumsy attempt to
attract attention from the opposite sex. Palm burglars winter
in the southern United States, especially Florida. And they will
mate in bogs. It's basically like an aging divorcé after a couple of
cocktails.

palm
burglar

Pine Shitkin

Common Name: Pine Siskin

These shits are brown and very streaky with subtle yellow edgings on their wings and tails, just like old underwear. They have a distinctive rising *"brzzzzzzt"* call that has been likened to the sound of slowly tearing a sheet of paper in half. This comparison is bullshit, though, because tearing paper is a soothing sound compared to the painfully high-pitched noises these jerks make. Imagine a marker running out of ink as it's dragged across a dry erase board, only 10x louder.

Color: *Yellow, shit streaks.*

pine
Shitkin

Tufted Titface

Common Name: Tufted Titmouse

This little gray jerk with his tufted jerk crest is common year-round in the eastern United States. Did you know that these fucks line their nests with hair, which they frequently yank right out of live animals? No joke—hair from dogs, cats, livestock, woodchucks, raccoons, even humans has been found in old nests. What the fuck?

Oh, and the little asshole has been busy expanding his range northward—he can now be found in woods, parks, and gardens as far north as southeastern Canada. Probably thanks to people putting bird feeders in their yards and providing a food supply. Nice job, everybody.

Identification: *Slate gray or gray above, lighter gray underparts. Stupid gray crest on its stupid gray head.*

tufted
titface

Western Meadowjerk

Common Name: Western Meadowlark

Look at this jerk, singing his heart out. The western meadowlark is a medium-sized Icterid bird, whatever that means. It builds its nest on the ground in open grasslands, which proves it's stupid. If you can fly, why the hell don't you build your nest in a tree where it's at least safe from dogs. Plus, it's the state bird of like six states you wouldn't want to live in.

western
Meadowjerk

Western Wood Pew-Pew

Common Name: Western Wood-Pewee

Small, plain, and drab, this uninspiring flycatcher of western woodlands is best known by its descending whistle. Its piercing, grating, descending whistle. The wood pew-pew sings at dawn—and at dusk. Oh, and late in the evening . . . when other songbirds have the common courtesy to shut the fuck up and give it a rest.

Note: *This species and the eastern wood-pewee look almost exactly alike, which makes you wonder, do these pewees lack a sense of individuality, or are they just both lazy about their appearance?*

Western
wood
Pew-Pew

White-breasted Butt Nugget

Common Name: White-breasted Nuthatch

An easy way to identify this dumb nuthatch is to look for the bird in your backyard that spends most of its time upside down. Its diet should be insects and acorns, but this bird is a sucker for free food, so they spend a lot of their time industriously carrying sunflower seeds away from your bird feeder to hide them in random crevices for shame-eating later, when nobody is watching.

Bird Note: *Their nasal calls are a familiar irritation on winter mornings over much of North America.*

white-breasted
Butt Nugget

Backyard Assholes

Damn Crows

Common Name: American Crow

Caw! Caw! Caw! Caw! Caw! Caw! Caw! Caw! Caw! Caw! Caw!
That's pretty much it with these jerks.

Dumb-Ass Robin

Common Name: American Robin

North America is freaking filled with these birds. You can see them pretty much everywhere without even trying, and they're easy to spot because you can't miss their dumb rust-red breast. The Latin name for the robin is *Turdus migratorius*. No joke. It gives you some idea of how beloved they are, because that means "Migrating Turd." On a positive note, they are a good food source for cats.

dumb-ass
robin

European Shartling

Common Name: European Starling

Pretty much everyone hates this unmusical bird. In urban areas they have huge roosts that cause noise problems, not to mention a giant mess of droppings. Farmers especially hate them because they will straight fuck up an orchard. To add insult to injury, the lazy pricks will eat your animal feed too. Black with gross pink legs.

Habitat: *Fucking everywhere.*

european
Shartling

Shit-Headed Cowbird

Common Name: Brown-headed Cowbird

These shit-heads are the worst. They lay eggs like it's going out of style. Seriously, like one every day, all summer long. The female finds the nest of some other bird, and she throws one of *their* eggs out of the nest. That's fucked up. Then she lays one of her own in its place and flies off laughing.

Shit-headed
cowbird

Stupid-Ass Steller's Jay

Common Name: Steller's Jay

This cocky motherfucker. While the Steller's jay does not have as prominent a crest as the Blue Jay, it is the only crested jay west of the Rocky Mountains, so it struts around the mountainous western forests like it's hot shit. It has a black head and deep-blue colored body, which you'd think would make it way hard to hide in evergreen trees, but this jay is so full of itself it's probably never considered hiding. Don't worry, though—if you do somehow manage to miss seeing their arrogant little blue bodies, you'll be sure to get an earful of their harsh, scolding calls if they're nearby.

Stupid-ASS
Steller's Jay

Hummingbirds, Weirdos, and Flycatchers

Butt-chinned Hummingbird

Common Name: Black-chinned Hummingbird

These tiny butt-faces are found in most of western North America. They have long bills and use their long extendable tongues to feed on nectar from wherever. They're basically the same as every other hummingbird.

Identification: *This one has metallic green back, glossy purple throat, and a black head, but if you've seen one hummingbird, you've seen them all.*

Butt-chinned
hummingbird

Doofus Hummingbird

Common Name: Rufous Hummingbird

I've heard them described as "the feistiest of all hummingbirds." I guess. These tiny assholes have a chip on their shoulder and will aggressively chase away other hummingbirds.

Tip: *They may take up residence in your garden if you put out a feeder, so don't.*

doofus
hummingbird

American Dickwood

Common Name: American Woodcock

This little dick is hard to see because he's colored like leaf litter. That's okay, though, because aside from its name, the woodcock is hardly worth mentioning. It's got a small fat body, short legs, and a big fat head. The eyes are set way too far back, making this bird look extra stupid. Probably so it can see while its weird flexible bill is jammed into the ground right up to its face trying to find worms.

Color: *Dirt*

Fact: *The American woodcock is colloquially referred to as a "timberdoodle." People also call it a "bogsucker," "mudsnipe," or "Labrador steamer." Nobody respects this bird.*

American
dickwood

Belted King-Pisser

Common Name: Belted Kingfisher

Look at this ridiculous fish-eating bird! Look how big his head is compared to his body! Hah! He kind of reminds me of Luis Guzmán, except that I like Luis Guzmán. Mr. Guzmán is a talented and underappreciated actor who can steal a scene with even a small part. This bird, on the other hand, eats fish and small amphibians by flying face-first into the water from a branch.

Hat Size: *Enormous*

belted
King-pisser

Fucking Pigeon

Common Name: Rock Pigeon

Oh my god, do I even need to talk about this bird?? They are tubby gray sacks-of-birdshit with tiny heads and short legs. You know this bird because they are fucking everywhere, shitting on everything.

Fun Fact: *Pigeons find their way home by using the Earth's magnetic fields, as well as the position of the sun, and who knows what else. Apparently, you can even blindfold these shits and they will still find their way back. What's even the point? Save your tiny blindfolds for some other bird, I guess.*

fucking
pigeon

Ass-throated Flycatcher

Common Name: Ash-throated Flycatcher

A passerine bird in the tyrant flycatcher family, this medium-sized ass of the Desert Southwest is known for its breeding season "Dawn Song" which, of course, it starts before dawn. This non-musical song is comprised of repeated high to low sounds, and the occasional "ha-wheeer." It sounds like it's blowing the notes through a wet whistle. It makes other annoying sounds throughout the rest of the day, in case you were wondering.

They are secondary cavity-nesters and will nest in basically any hole they find, so rev your engine a few times in the morning to blow out any nests that might have been made in your tailpipe. Also, if you hang your laundry to dry, check your pants before you put them on. These guys are idiots.

Color: *Pale yellow belly and brown tail feathers are probably meant to help it blend into its desert surroundings, but it mostly looks like this bird needs to be run through the wash.*

Ass-throated
flycatcher

Fuck-tailed Flycatcher

Common Name: Fork-tailed Flycatcher

Haha, look at this dumbshit's tail. A wanderer from the tropics, it shows up almost every year in North America, reaching as far as the northeastern seaboard. It's impossible to predict where they will show up, though, because most fork-tailed flycatchers reaching us have come from southern South America and were headed for Mexico. What a fuck-up. This bird can't even do basic bird things right.

fuck-tailed
flycatcher

Egotists and Show-offs

American Redfart

Common Name: American Redstart

Deep black with vibrant flashes of orange on the wings, flank, and tail, these medium-sized warblers could almost be mistaken for fat butterflies, if only they would shut up and calm down for a minute. But these hyperactive twits are perpetually shooting back and forth through the bushes trying to catch some bug, or prancing down a branch, rapidly fanning their black and orange tails open and closed in an attempt to startle more bugs into flight.

Sadly, they are also much noisier than butterflies. The song of the males (five or more rapidly repeated notes, often ending in an upward or downward accented phrase) is loud, high pitched, and could be described as sneeze-like. Or, fart-like, if you're being honest.

Backyard Tip: *While they feed primarily on insects, an abundance of small fruits and berries will attract these birds in late summer. So if you plant bushes or trees of this nature in your yard, be forewarned. I think we can all agree, no one wants to have redfarts.*

American
RedFart

Eastern Kingbutt

Common Name: Eastern Kingbird

This big-headed dope looks like he's wearing a business suit. A medium-sized songbird of eastern North America, this kingbird is notable for his stiff, upright posture of self-importance common to many business-types.

Identification: *Dark gray upper parts. Crisp white throat, chest, and abdomen, with just a bit of cuff showing at the tail. Probably heavy starch. Thinks he's better than you.*

Eastern
Kingbutt

Red-winged Buttwad

Common Name: Red-winged Blackbird

This blackbird is extremely abundant in North America, so you've probably already spotted one of these assholes sitting on a cattail, flaunting its gaudy shoulder markings. Territorial and full of themselves, the males make a big deal out of trying to get noticed during breeding season by nasally shrieking their "CONK-ah-SKwEEE" song, over and over, from every damp field and soggy roadside.

The buttwads in northern North America migrate to the southern United States. Southern and some lazy western populations don't migrate at all. Interestingly, who cares, because they're already everywhere. Also, during winter these bastards congregate in flocks as large as several million to eat grains. Nobody needs this. I mean, really. Find your own thing, buttwad, because we already have starlings for this shit.

Identifying the female: *A nondescript brown and easily mistaken for, like, a million other drab birds, so not really worth it.*

Red-winged
buttwad

Scarlet Teenager

Common Name: Scarlet Tanager

What is it with these tanagers? The males are possibly the most unnecessarily red birds in any eastern forest. They stay high in the forest canopy all summer long (doing god knows what) and then in the fall they just take off for South America. But not before inexplicably changing from red feathers to yellow-green feathers (which, by the way, makes them look just like the yellow-green females). I don't know what they're up to, but I don't like it and somebody ought to do something about it.

Scarlet
Teenager

Western Kingbutt

Common Name: Western Kingbird

The eye-catching color combination of a light gray upper half and bright lemon-yellow under-parts makes this medium-sized member of the tyrant flycatcher family easy to spot when perched upright on fences or power lines.

You would think, being from the west, this bird would be much mellower than its eastern kingbird counterpart. Nope. This one is just as much of a dick in its own way, sputtering angry vocalizations, wing-flapping, and aggressively chasing off any other birds it sees as a threat.

Did you know? *The kingbird gets its name from its grandiose behavior when defending its territory—they are known to chase away larger predatory birds because they are too self-entitled to realize they are meant to be hawk food.*

Western Kingbutt

Fuckers

Northern Fucker

Common Name: Northern Flicker

This bastard is a medium-sized member of the woodpecker family, native to most of North America, plus some parts of Central America and even Cuba. Apparently, it's one of the few woodpeckers that migrates, so there's no getting away from the hammering of its stupid beak on old trees. It's how they get at grubs and beetles or whatever.

Color: *Some red junk on its face, but mostly beige with stupid spots.*

northern
fucker

Pileated Woodfucker

Common Name: Pileated Woodpecker

This is a large woodpecker whose drumming on dead trees or utility poles can be heard from blocks away. Usually early in the morning when you're trying to enjoy a little peace and quiet. It always seems to echo in the morning stillness for some reason, so if one of these assholes is looking for carpenter ants or termites, you'll know about it.

Color: *Mainly black with a ridiculous red crest on its head.*

pileated
woodfucker

Red-breasted Shitsucker

Common Name: Red-breasted Sapsucker

These shit suckers can be found at low or middle elevations in the coniferous forests of the northern Pacific Coast. Its piercing and screamlike *"EEEAHH!!"* call is enough to stop your heart if you're not expecting it, but what will really get on your nerves is the drumming: a slow, irregular knocking that's indistinguishable from a rhythmically challenged kid banging on a tree with a stick.

Feeding: *Most woodpeckers have the decency to drill dead trees, but this fucker drills holes all over live trees so it can suck the sap. It keeps coming back to feed and may even kill the tree over time—it's like some kind of goddamned tree vampire.*

red-breasted
shitsucker

Floaters, Sandbirds, and Dork-legs

Common Goon

Common Name: Common Loon

They stick out like dumbasses. In the summertime you might see bunch of these big black and white fish-divers just floating around in the middle of a lake. It's like a car full of guys in tuxedos slowly cruising a strip mall parking lot after hours: suspicious.

Note: *Creepy red eyes.*

Common Goon

Dullard

Common Name: Mallard

If someone is feeding bread to a bunch of ducks at a park, chances are this bread-hog is in the scuffle shoving other ducks out of the way to get it. The dullard can be found throughout the Northern and Southern Hemispheres probably because people feed them bread wherever they go. Slightly heavier than other members of the duck family, it has a striking bottle-green head and could be a very pretty bird if it just lost some weight. All that bread, though.

dullard

Goddamned Canada Goose

Common Name: Canada Goose

Thanks a lot, Canada. These fuckers are often considered a pest species. Why? Because of their depredation of crops, their noise, droppings, aggressive behavior, and habit of begging for food in urban parks, not to mention that incessant honking, and their long, stupid necks. Basically, everything about these geese just makes you want to choke them.

Goose Tips: *Feeding the geese at the park? Be aware that they can become overly aggressive in large groups. If you have to fight, don't let them surround you—keep moving and try to take them on individually or in small groups.*

god damnped
Canoda
goose

Caspian Turd

Common Name: Caspian Tern

This big son of a bitch is the biggest tern in North America. The aggressive shits are known for inflicting bloody wounds on the heads of people who accidentally wander into their territory on the beach. But if a single bald eagle flies overhead, the entire colony will take flight and leave the chicks to be eaten by gulls.

Identification: *Bright coral-red bill, poor parenting.*

Caspian
Turd

Seadull

Common Name: Seagull

If you live near the coast, these sons of bitches are everywhere. Also, if you live near a garbage dump. Gulls don't care whether they're eating a small marine invertebrate or a rancid french fry from the trash. They enjoy eating garbage and shitting everywhere.

Scientifically speaking, gulls belong to the family *Laridae*, which are seabirds in the order *Charadriiformes*. The commonly used term "seagull" is actually a catch-all for the many different types of gull and doesn't describe a specific bird. Practically speaking, this doesn't matter because they're all the same trash bird at heart.

Did you know? *The California gull (Larus californicus) doesn't even represent its namesake, California; the best it could do, apparently, was state bird of Utah.*

Seagull

Great Blue Moron

Common Name: Great Blue Heron

This big moron is found throughout North America. It's usually standing shin-deep in the water like an idiot. The largest of the North American morons, it's always trying to choke some giant fish down its stupid neck. There are plenty of other fish that would fit.

great blue **Moron**

Limpdick
Common Name: Limpkin

This weird dick of the hot southern swamps only makes it as far north as Florida during the breeding season and forages almost exclusively on apple snails. It has a weird bill that's long and a little gapped near the tip, and it curves slightly to the right. Some claim that this is perfectly normal, and that actually it can be better than a straight one, because you can, you know, really, um . . . get it all up into those right-chambered snail shells . . . ugh.

Oh, and if that didn't give you the creeps, this bird is a screamer, and it's sometimes called the "crying bird." It's like this bird is made of bad one-night stands.

Identification: *Long neck. Long legs. Long curved bill. Sad and creepy.*

Limpdick

Solitary Sand-pooper

Common Name: Solitary Sandpiper

Pretty much all sandpipers migrate in flocks and nest on the ground, but not this dickweed. It is usually found alone, along the bank of some shitty creek. If approached, it bobs nervously, then flies away. Rather than nesting on the ground like a normal sandpiper, this turd lays its eggs in old songbird nests up in the trees. Fucking weirdo.

Identification: *Pale-spotted, dark brown back and rump, dark head, streaks on—fuck it, who cares.*

Solitary
Sand pooper

Wood Snork

Common Name: Wood Stork

These big bald-headed wading birds are the only member of the stork family that breeds in the United States. More importantly, they really creep me the fuck out. Legs like long black sticks with weird pink feet; skin on their featherless heads formed into small scale-like plates; gross rumple-skinned turkey-necks the size of a baby's arm. Ugh. And they are mostly silent *except for their hissing and bill clappering*. What kind of bird fucking *hisses*?

Habitat: *Southeastern swamps, nightmares.*

Wood Snork

Murder birds

Crested Chacha

Common Name: Crested Caracara

Sometimes called the *Northern Crested Caracara* or *Audubon's Crested Caracara*, this big lazy son of a bitch should have its bird-of-prey-license revoked, because it mainly feeds on carrion. When they bother to catch live prey, it's usually immobile or incapacitated already. You'd think a member of the *Falconidae* family could make more of an effort. Also, "crested"? I don't think so—that dollar-store toupee isn't fooling anyone.

Notes: *Dopey long legs, flat-talons, embarrassment to real raptors.*

crested
~~caracara~~
c~~aract~~
chacha

Great Grey Shite

Common Name: Great Grey Shrike

This ice-cold motherfucker is what's called a "predatory songbird." It really should be called a "Murder-Bird" because the homicidal little shrike feeds on small mammals and other birds and, I swear I am not making this up, often impales them on thorns or barbed wire fences. That is some sick shit right there. Its scientific name, *Lanius excubitor*, literally means "sentinel butcher."

Bonus Fact: *If you look into the cold, black abyss of their eyes you can see evil.*

great grey
shite

Motherfucking Bald Eagle

Common Name: Bald Eagle

Is this bird flawed? Hell, yes—it's a bird. But it stands for the *promise* of something good. Please, don't even get me started, because this is the best motherfucking bird there is. Period.

motherfucking
BALD
EAGLE

Pooper's Hawk

Common Name: Cooper's Hawk

A medium-sized hawk named after New York naturalist William Cooper, who founded an academy or something. You'd probably be proud of this, if you were some prig 19th century naturalist. Of course, this bird is also commonly called a chicken hawk, hen hawk, quail hawk, and, I'm not even joking, a "big blue darter," so don't let it go to your head, Cooper.

This dumb bird of prey feeds on smaller birds and relies on stealth attacks from covered perches within the trees—which means flying through dense vegetation at high speeds—to catch its prey. Sounds pretty badass, until you imagine a hawk flying into a branch. Scientists have studied a lot of their skeletons and found about a quarter of them have broken bones in their chests.

Backyard Tip: *If you put out seed for birds in your backyard, you may also attract the attention of a Cooper's Hawk looking for a meal. This is nature's way of making up for how annoying songbirds are.*

pooper's
hawk

Section 3:
Tips for Watching Birds

Whether you're new to watching birds, or you've managed to suffer through it for years, here are a few things I've found that help to make birding suck a little less.

#1: Get some Binoculars.
This one is obvious. Without binoculars, you're just some loser sitting in the bushes.

#2: Invest in a decent thermos and stay comfortable.
Okay, you've got your binoculars and your thermos of hot coffee! You're ready for a morning of bird watching, right? No. Let's be honest, this shit is boring as hell. You might as well put some booze in that thermos. Whether you're going to be sitting outdoors for hours on end, or just staring out your kitchen window, it helps to be a little drunk.

#3: Carry a notebook.
You might want to record your bird sightings and make notes on what you observe for later, like which birds shit on your patio furniture, because one day there will be a reckoning. Mark my words.

#4: Always ask for permission before entering private property. ALWAYS.
Maybe you are innocently wearing binoculars and crouching in someone's bushes without permission. Maybe they just immediately assume that you are some kind of pervert and totally freak out. Maybe they pretty much won't even listen to you at this point, so don't even bother trying to explain. Typical!

· Also, you'd be surprised at how quickly rural police can respond in these situations, so it's definitely worth it to ask the property owner's permission in advance. Trust me on this one.

#5: Get a good field guide.
Oh, wait, you already have one in your hand, so I guess you can check this one off your list. But you might also have a friend or relative who is becoming interested in bird watching. There are ways to tell, if you know what to look for. For instance, when seeing a bird, do they appear to give a shit what kind of bird it is? Do them a favor and buy them a copy of this book.

#6: Get knowledgeable.

If you're going to go out and be surrounded by birds, it's probably a good idea to know as much as you can about them. For instance, did you know that geese can be very aggressive and are generally shitty? A knowledgeable bird watcher would never let themselves be surrounded by these assholes. They are horrible and have no redeeming qualities.

#7: Learn about your camera.

Up until quite recently a quality camera and lens were limited to the realm of professional photographers and those few amateur enthusiasts willing to pay a significant amount of money for them. But today more and more people carry a smartphone with them wherever they go. The cameras in these phones are constantly being improved by the manufacturers and are now capable of capturing amazing high-resolution images. This won't help you, though, because the amazing camera in your amazing phone has complete shit for a lens. For the purpose of photographing birds it is essentially useless because *it was designed for taking selfies*. You should probably just stick to doing that anyway.

Feud for thought: Many serious birders disapprove of bird photographers, believing that they would go to any length to get that perfect photo, even if it is disruptive to the birds (and merely for the sake of garnering more Facebook likes, I'm sure). On the other hand, many bird photographers don't care much for serious birders or their pompous snobbery. Either way the feud between these two camps is stupid, because face it, birds hate us all.

#8: Find other local birders.

Becoming a member of the local birding club, or just casually getting to know other bird watchers in your area, can be a valuable way to increase your bird knowledge and bird enjoyment quickly—finding out where the weekend birding hotspots are or who the local sparrow expert is may help you dodge these passionate enthusiasts in the field and avoid an exhausting conversation about social behaviors common to birds of the *Passer* genus.

Section 4:

Four Seasons of Bird Watching

Spring

All across North America, one of the surest signs that spring is here is the return of the migratory birds.

One morning you wake up and the trees around you are suddenly filled with all sorts of dumb singing birds that were not there yesterday. Incredibly, many of these birds have flown thousands of miles to reach your yard, following only celestial and magnetic cues passed down genetically.

Nobody invited them, but there they are anyway.

Spring Birding Tip: *It's spring, so really just walk into any plot of trees and look up. Many songbirds become quite active first thing in the morning as the sun's rays warm things up and create insect activity. This bullshit can make sleeping past dawn almost impossible, but birds don't care because they don't have any respect for those of us with jobs.*

Summer

Ah, those long lazy days of summer. We all crave a little rest and relaxation this time of year, am I right? But if you were planning to take a vacation from the never-ending chitter and prattle of your avian antagonists, think again, because there's no getting away from them. And you might as well forget that nice summer boat ride, because birds are everywhere along rivers and shorelines this time of year.

Summer Birding Tip: *What a great time of year to stretch out in a hammock strung between two trees and relax with a tall glass of iced tea while you gaze up into the branches. Just keep an eye on your glass, because you don't want to sip down any bird shit. Actually, watch your eyes, because they'll shit in those, too. Take my word for it.*

Fall

Autumn is a popular time for watching birds. The warm weather and carefree fun of summer may be gone, but those chirpy little bastards are still hanging around.

One thing to keep in mind is that many birds scout their winter food sources in fall, deciding which backyards they will shit in all winter. (This is in part due to the increased difficulty of finding food in the wild during winter, but also because birds lack determination and self-respect.)

If a bird discovers that your yard is worth visiting now, they'll remember later. A bird feeder or some seed on the ground is all it takes; you will never get rid of them.

Fall Birding Tip: *Hot apple cider with whiskey makes it all easier. Heat apple cider in a pan on the stove until hot. Pour 2 ounces of your favorite whiskey into a mug and—actually, you might as well make it 3 ounces if you're going to have to watch birds prancing around your yard all day. Top with cider (optional).*

Winter

I love the onset of winter, especially those perfect days when it's clear and cold outside, the sun peeks through trees bare of leaves, and there's a delicate dusting of frost on the ground. The air is crisp and still, and everything seems happily at peace, at least until the graceless honking of some migrating ducks fuck it all up.

If you are new to bird watching, I have bad news for you: winter is not the off-season. Depending on where you live, you are likely to be bothered even in your own backyard by any number of grosbeaks, juncos, and all kinds of hungry chattering finches, chickadees and cardinals, not to mention whatever various noisy waterfowl are passing overhead.

Winter Birding Tip: *Stay inside. (Put some black oil sunflower seeds on the ground outside, or hang a feeder in view of your window, then make yourself a hot toddy. At least you can enjoy staying warm while those greedy little bastards mooch off you in the freezing cold outside.)*

FALL MIGRATION

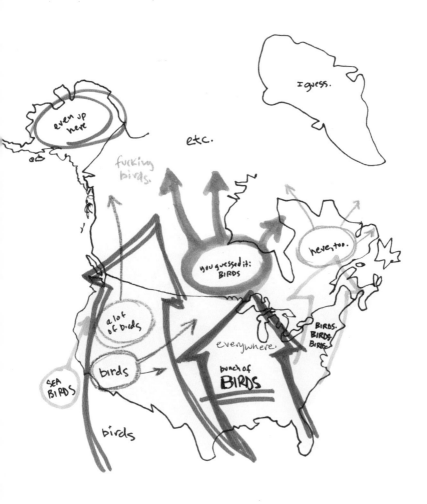

SPRING MIGRATION

Section 5:
Extinct Species

While the focus of this book is squarely on the world of living birds that can be observed in nature, it would be somewhat remiss to pass up the opportunity to highlight a few special North American birds that were too dumb to survive in the modern world. I'm not talking prehistoric creatures here, but birds that were around a couple hundred years ago and just couldn't muster the resolve to continue existing. Of course, who can blame them, really?

Carolina Parakreep

Common Name: Carolina Parakeet

This small green putz with the bright-yellow head and orange face was the only parrot indigenous to the United States. Living in swamps or old growth along rivers, they were at one time a dime a dozen, found from New York to the Great Plains, and down to the Gulf of Mexico. But by the mid-1800s its numbers were becoming thin.

It lived in noisy flocks of up to 300 birds, and its diet was made up of mostly seeds from trees and shrubs. But this fucking guy had a real penchant for toxic cockleburs, so it was in fact a poison parrot, and cats who ate them frequently died. Damn, but way to take one for the team, cats.

Deforestation probably had a lot to do with their decline, but they were also hunted extensively for their colorful feathers. The flocking behavior that reportedly led these colorful dumbfucks back to the scene of other dead and dying parrots who were being shot by hunters probably did not help them either.

The last known Carolina parakeet expired in captivity in 1918 in the Cincinnati Zoo, but the species was not declared officially extinct until 1939. They probably just wanted to make sure.

Notes: *Do not eat.*

Great Ugh

Common Name: Great Auk

Standing almost three feet tall and weighing over ten pounds, this big penguin-looking motherfucker must have been something to see. It was found in the cold north Atlantic waters and what we know of its behavior is almost entirely limited to observations made by sailors, not scientists.

While similar in appearance, they are unrelated to the penguin, who may have gained its name from the great auk's scientific genus, *Pinguinus*. In fact the word "penguin" appeared in the 16th century as a synonym for Auk. 18th century whalers did not give a single fuck and referred to both as "woggins." Ships' logs from the time noted them as being quite fatty and delicious, but 18th century whalers would eat just about anything. Apparently, they also made great fires if you didn't have wood available.

While the species isn't believed to have gone entirely extinct until 1852, what is thought to be the last great auk in the British Isles was captured in 1844 on an islet in Scotland and then beaten to death with sticks by three men who believed the auk to be a witch responsible for the appearance of a large storm. This might have been the unluckiest bird ever.

great
ugh

Labrador Dunce

Common Name: Labrador Duck

Not a lot is actually known about this this beady-eyed sea duck, which was already rare when Europeans first noticed it. This mysterious fuck was alleged to have bred in Labrador (hence the name), but no one really knows for sure where the dummies originated. They appeared from Nova Scotia to New Jersey, but John James Audubon's son John Woodhouse reported seeing a nest in Labrador. It turns out what he actually saw was an empty nest, or maybe just a pile of sticks, but he claimed that some guy he talked to said it belonged to a Labrador duck at some time. Not what I would call conclusive evidence, but apparently it was good enough for John Woodhouse and his dad, so whatever.

These ducks were hunted, but not really all that much, because people generally agreed that they tasted awful. They were basically inedible, so we can assume that anyone shooting a Labrador duck must have had personal reasons.

They were already on their way out as a species by the mid 1800s, and the last one was recorded in 1878. The exact cause for their extinction is unclear, but there's really no reason for this duck to remain in existence anyway.

Labrador
dunce

Passenger Pudgen

Common Name: Passenger Pigeon

This nomadic pigeon was found more or less everywhere east of the Rocky Mountains in North America until about the beginning of the 20th century. They weren't as fat as their small heads made them look, but they were still considered cheap eats, especially in the 19th century when they were hunted on a massive scale for decades, and their numbers rapidly declined in the late 1800s.

This bird's voice was described as unmusical, loud, and made up of harsh clucks, low cooing, and croaks. Apparently, large flocks could be deafening and heard for miles. No one is saying it's related, but the last wild Passenger Pigeon was shot in 1901.

Description: *Ugly and pigeony. Blueish grayish-gray, with some rusty brownish.*

passenger
pudgeon

Section 6:

Bird Feeders

It should go without saying, but be warned that if you choose to put a bird feeder in your yard, you are probably going to attract a bunch of birds. That may seem like a good idea in the moment, but believe me, once the lazy bastards figure out that there's a free meal to be had, they will just keep showing up hungry and expecting a handout. But go for it, if you like being taken advantage of. There are a multitude of types and styles of bird feeders available—far too many to mention all of them, but here are the basics.

Choosing the right feeder

When choosing a feeder, you may wish to consult with your local National Audubon Society chapter or local birding club about what types bird feeders are most appropriate for your region, which birds are attracted to the various types of feeders, what types of feed are preferred by the various local species, and so on. But the bird nerds will probably want to give you an earful, so you may want to do your own research; there is an abundance of information available on the internet. If that all seems tedious, just choose one at random and fill it with seed, because most birds will eat out of anything.

Tray or Platform Feeder

If you're unsure where to begin, you might consider this type of feeder. It's the simplest type, is easy to maintain, and attracts a wide variety of birds, like finches, jays, sparrows, really anything that can stand on a raised tray of food and gobble seed. Most birds are shamelessly messy eaters, so they're going to knock a lot of the food off the tray, but don't worry, because all the spilled seed is going to attract the ground feeders like juncos and goldfinches. Of course the open design is also going to make this an easy-access buffet for squirrels, raccoons, and any deer of average or better height, so congratulations, now you're feeding the whole goddamned neighborhood.

GLUTTONOUS FREELOADER

SEED

TRAY

STAND

GROUND

(height: frustratingly out of-reach for most cats.)

Suet Feeder

Suet is hard fat from beef or mutton. Mixed with birdseed, it provides a high-fat, high-protein food source for birds during harsh winter months. You can purchase a suet feeder, which is usually a wire cage of some sort, but it's easy and inexpensive to make your own natural pinecone feeder. Find a pinecone that is fairly open; larger ones may be easier to work with. Spread the suet on the cone, pressing it into the gaps between scales. Now coat the cone in birdseed (you may need to press it in to make sure it adheres to the fat) and hang it with a piece of twine.

Note: *Touching suet is kind of gross. Also, the mental image of a hoard of birds gleefully gorging themselves on raw animal fat in a bleak winter landscape is shudder-inducing, so you can substitute peanut butter if you like. Plus, imagine a bird trying to chirp with a big beakful of extra-crunchy.*

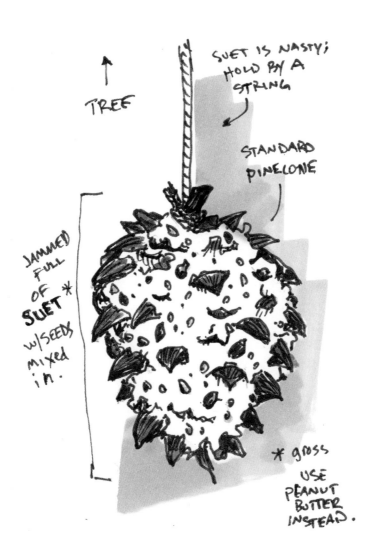

TREE

SUET IS NASTY;
HOLD BY A
STRING

STANDARD
PINECONE

JAMMED
FULL
OF
SUET *
w/SEEDS
MiXeD
in.

* gross
USE
PEANUT
BUTTER
INSTEAD.

Tube Feeder

This is a type of hanging feeder that is filled with seed and allows feeding through screens or ports in the tube, which do a somewhat decent job of protecting the food from the elements. Some high-end models include special hoods to discourage squirrels, but squirrels are smarter than you think, so don't get depressed when they figure out how to loot your expensive anti-squirrel bird feeder. Tube feeders often incorporate small perches for the small perching birds, which helps alleviate competition from larger bird jerks like jays. Those guys are pushy assholes.

Make your own tube feeder: *If you don't want to spring for an expensive tube feeder and don't care what your yard looks like, apparently you can easily make your own from a discarded plastic soda bottle. Some people call this "upcycling" because it makes them feel okay about hanging trash from their tree branches.*

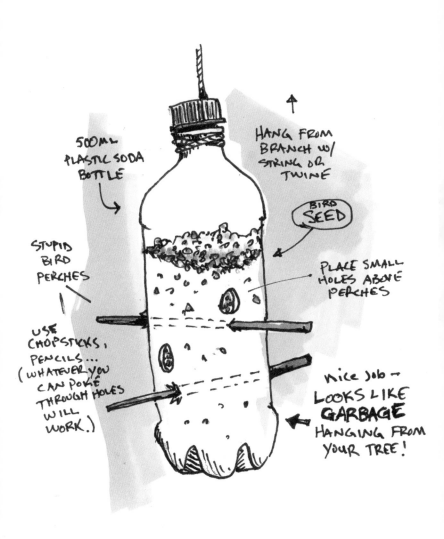

500ML PLASTIC SODA BOTTLE

HANG FROM BRANCH w/ STRING OR TWINE

BIRD SEED

PLACE SMALL HOLES ABOVE PERCHES

STUPID BIRD PERCHES

USE CHOPSTICKS, PENCILS... (WHATEVER YOU CAN POKE THROUGH HOLES WILL WORK.)

nice Job — LOOKS LIKE **GARBAGE** HANGING FROM YOUR TREE!

House or Hopper Feeder

These enclosed feeders are essentially a gravity-fed seed hopper. While they protect the seed better than tray feeders, house feeders do require more effort, since they must be emptied, cleaned, and allowed to dry out at least once a month. For some reason everyone who makes house feeders seems compelled to design them to look like a real house of some sort. With some effort, you can even find or build one to match the architectural style of your home. Of course, birds are too dumb to appreciate architectural consistency, and your friends will think you have a high opinion of yourself when they see that you've installed a tiny matching Cape Cod in your yard. Probably better to stick with a basic model.

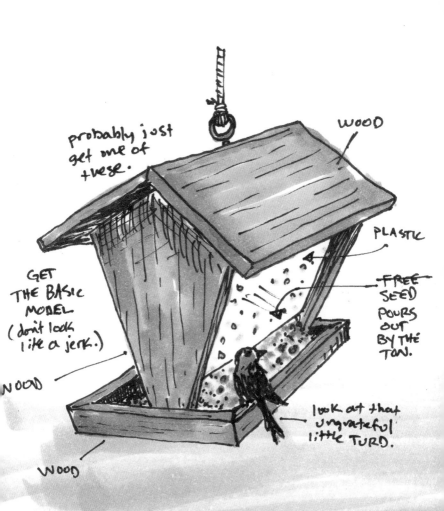

probably just get one of these.

WOOD

PLASTIC

GET THE BASIC MODEL (don't look like a jerk.)

FREE SEED POURS OUT BY THE TON.

WOOD

WOOD

look at that ungrateful little TURD.

Section 7:

Keeping Your Own Bird Journal

Why keep a bird journal?

Naturalists and ornithologists have long kept field journals of their thoughts, drawings, and observations to be used for later reference and as an aid to their scholarly pursuit of knowledge. But in recent years, more and more normal people are taking up journaling as a pastime too.

There are many ways and reasons to keep a journal, and keeping a bird journal can be a rewarding endeavor. You may want to keep track of the birds you see over time, along with notes on their appearance, location, movements, and behaviors. This makes identification easier in the long run, and will build your familiarity with the birds that frequent the area. The F.B.I. keeps dossiers on criminals, don't they?

Journals vs. Field Notes

There's actually quite a bit of overlap between field notes and journals in terms of what is included in them, but there is a difference in their intended use.

Field notes are qualitative notes taken by researchers in the field and are generally intended to document for the purpose of identification or data collection. Notes on markings, postures, flight behavior, calls, location, etc. are all typically recorded in field notes, as well as sketches or drawings that visually capture what is observed.

Bird journals, on the other hand, may contain many of the same types of observations and drawings, but are more personal and reflective in nature. They are intended to document your experiences with birds and facilitate a deeper understanding of the little pissants.

A note on using the proper term: *I suggest "journal," but if you are making notes about the birds you see, it's pretty safe to use either term, since generally only researchers are invested in the distinction, and only the most didactic would bring it up in conversation. If you do find yourself called out on this point by some tedious academic, please know that you are now morally obligated to smile and give them the middle finger.*

How to start your bird journal

There's really no "right way" to journal. It is a record of what you see and think. If you're not sure where to start, you may find it helpful to decide on a few basic pieces of info and record them for each bird you see. You will find yourself expanding on this as you get comfortable with journaling.

You might start by simply noting the date, time, and location where the bird was seen, and then try to make a sketch of the bird. Try to see and note details about the bird, such as size, color, and markings. In no time you will naturally move on to jotting notes about how it behaved like an asshole, what kind of nerve-racking call it made, or the look of blank stupidity in its eyes, etc.

Tools and tips for writing and drawing in the field

1. You need some kind of notebook to write in. People use everything from three-ring binders to sketchbooks to composition notebooks. I recommend something small enough to carry in a pocket if you'll be taking notes out in the field. And durable, because nature is a bitch.

2. You need something to write with. Like a pen or a pencil. Whatever. I shouldn't have to tell you this. Any writing implement will work, but if you think you are some kind of artist, a lot of people like adding watercolors to their pencil or ink drawings. It's okay to do your initial drawing in the field and then go back and add color later. In fact, one could argue it's better that way, because you look like an idiot stumbling through the woods with your hands full of paints and brushes. But if you don't mind the other birders laughing behind your back, then go right ahead. I recommend a pocket-sized portable watercolor kit, because maybe you won't look so obvious.

3. Don't worry about spelling. Whether you share it with others or not, this journal is really for you. If *you* know what you're talking about, then who cares about spelling? If you're like me, you can't even read your own writing half the time, so grammar probably doesn't matter, either.

4. Waterproof paper allows you to journal in the rain. I'll be honest with you, though, bird journaling in the rain is miserable. Also, waterproof paper tends to be fairly expensive. It's mostly for scientists and show-offs.

5. Find a quiet spot to sit and observe. Take some time to sit down and really observe the birds. Drawing and writing is a great way to train your eye to see the details. Believe me, after a while, you will want to capture for posterity everything you can about these shifty little pricks, because someone needs to.

6. You can't mess it up. Don't worry if your drawing is terrible. Remember, this journal is a record of your journey into the world of bird watching; it is part of a learning process and doesn't need to be perfect. For me, it's less important to render a bird in perfect detail than to capture the feeling of its true shittiness.

The following are a few examples from my own field journal pages, which I hope will serve to make the process less mysterious and perhaps inspire you to keep your own record of the birds you see and how they have affected you and your appreciation for nature.

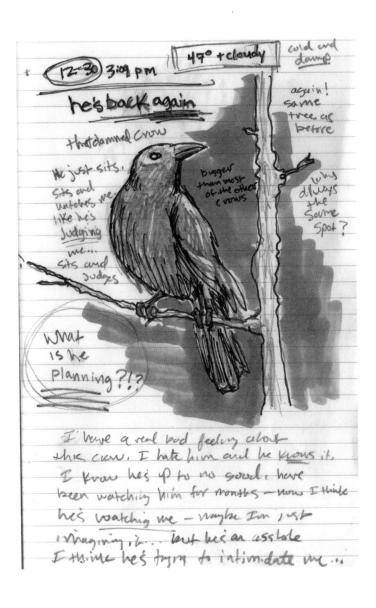

12-30 3:09 pm   47° + cloudy   cold and damp

he's back again

again! same tree as before

that damned crow

He just sits.
Sits and
watches me.
like he's
Judging
me...
Sits and
Judges

bigger than most of the other crows

why always the same spot?

What
is he
Planning ?!?

I have a real bad feeling about
this crow, I hate him and he knows it.
I know he's up to no good, have
been watching him for months — now I think
he's watching me — maybe I'm just
imagining it... but he's an asshole
I think he's trying to intimidate me...

.28
Hot! 80°+

not much happening today
too hot I think.

Saw a couple of birds
loitering in the back yard.

fatso

"Chestnuts' here is
one of them ——→
fucking chickadees — you could
tell he thinks his cute

* Call garbage company !!!

9/29
COLD SNAP   WTF? 63°F

these temp drop since
yesterday — yard is littered
with these little jerks
today, all prancing
around

were did they
all come from?

Total
Attitude.

chestnuts pack chickadees

Everywhere !!!

XI-12 (55°) LOTS OF RAIN

RAINING off and on for
several days — fair amount
of activity from various
birds (They never take a break)

Lot of bird noise from the
trees and brush down
the edge of the hill...

Can't make out what it
is, but its an infernal
racket. Going to investigate
further.

Fence
YARD
BIRD
NOISE

trees
brush

HILL

(continued)

Rain picked up suddenly —
pretty slippery on the
hill Bad fall — thank
god that tree stopped
my fall or I think
I would have gone all
the way off. Took
me 15 minutes to get
back up out of the bushes

didn't get a good look
what kind of
bird?

whole
bunch of
these assholes
back there
in the trees.

laughing
at me.

Acknowledgments

To Randy, who laughed at the first bird drawing, and got the joke right away.

To my agent, Rosie, who found me, believed in me, and convinced everyone to take a chance on me.

To my editor, Becca, and everyone at Chronicle who helped and guided me as this collection of short form musings was forged into a book.

And most of all, to my wife, Gina, whose love never ebbs, and whose support while writing this has never faltered, from the moment I sheepishly admitted that I had "sort of kind of accidentally created a blog about dumb birds with thousands of followers (oh, did I not mention that before?) well anyway, now I think I might be writing a book...", through the many nights and the weekends spent writing it.

Thank you for the opportunity, support, and help. This has been amazing and rewarding experience, and I am grateful to you all, because you made it possible.

References

American Birding Association. "American Birding Association Code of Birding Ethics"
listing.aba.org/ethics/

Birdwatching.com. www.birdwatching.com

The Cornell Lab of Ornithology. All About Birds. www.allaboutbirds.org/

The Cornell Lab of Ornithology. Project FeederWatch. feederwatch.org/

Giaimo, Cara. "What's A Woggin? A Bird, a Word, and a Linguistic Mystery." *Atlas Obscura*. www.atlasobscura.com/articles/whats-a-woggin-a-bird-a-word-and-a-linguistic-mystery

Mayntz, Melissa. "What Types of Sounds Do Birds Make?" *The Spruce*. www.thespruce.com/what-types-of-sounds-do-birds-make-387332

National Audubon Society. Guide to North American Birds. www.audubon.org/bird-guide

National Geographic. National Geographic Animals. www.nationalgeographic.com/animals/

NWNature.net. Birds of the Pacific Northwest. nwnature.net/birds/

Rainier Audubon Society. www.rainieraudubon.org/

Reader's Digest Editors. *Book of North American Birds*. Pleasantville, N.Y. Reader's Digest Association. 1990.

Seattle Audubon Society. *BirdWeb*. www.birdweb.org/birdweb/

WhatBird. www.whatbird.com/

Wikipedia. en.wikipedia.org/